DATE DUE

HATSHEPSUT

EGYPT'S FIRST FEMALE PHARAOH

SPECIAL LIVES IN HISTORY THAT BECOME

Signature LIVES

HATSHEPSUT

EGYPT'S FIRST FEMALE PHARAOH

by Pamela Dell

Content Adviser: Kathlyn M. Cooney, Ph.D.,
Egyptologist, Getty Research Institute

Reading Adviser: Rosemary G. Palmer, Ph.D.,
Department of Literacy, College of Education,
Boise State University

Compass Point Books ✦ Minneapolis, Minnesota

Compass Point Books
151 Good Counsel Drive
P.O. Box 669
Mankato, MN 56002-0669

 This book was manufactured with paper containing at least
10 percent post-consumer waste.

Editor: Anthony Wacholtz
Page Production: Bobbie Nuytten
Photo Researcher: Svetlana Zhurkin
Cartographer: XNR Productions, Inc.
Library Consultant: Kathleen Baxter

Art Director: LuAnn Ascheman-Adams
Creative Director: Keith Griffin
Editorial Director: Nick Healy
Managing Editor: Catherine Neitge

Library of Congress Cataloging-in-Publication Data
Dell, Pamela.
 Hatshepsut : Egypt's first female pharaoh / by Pamela Dell.
   p. cm.—(Signature lives)
 Includes bibliographical references and index.
 ISBN 978-0-7565-3835-4 (library binding)
1. Hatshepsut, Queen of Egypt—Juvenile literature. 2. Egypt—
History—Eighteenth dynasty, ca. 1570–1320 B.C.—Juvenile literature.
3. Pharaohs—Biography—Juvenile literature. I. Title. II. Series.
 DT87.15.D45 2008
 932'.014092—dc22
 [B]   2008005721

Visit Compass Point Books on the Internet at *www.compasspointbooks.com*
or e-mail your request to *custserv@compasspointbooks.com*

ANCIENT WORLD

Societies of long ago were peopled with unique men and women who would make their mark on the world. As we learn more and more about them, we continue to marvel at their accomplishments. We enjoy their works of art and literature. And we acknowledge that their beliefs, their actions, and their lives led to the world we know today. These men and women would make—and change—history.

Table of Contents

Chapter

1 A UNIQUE LEADER

❧❧❧

Thousands of years ago, Egypt was the land of the pharaohs, powerful kings who ruled without question. One of the most exceptional pharaohs ever to rule Egypt was virtually unknown until the mid-1800s. Here was a new name—Hatshepsut—that the modern world had never heard of. The more the archaeologists found out about this pharaoh, who ruled approximately 3,500 years ago, the more the mystery seemed to deepen.

Hatshepsut had spent at least 20 years on the throne during the early New Kingdom. She had governed during a time of peace, initiating a grand-scale building program. She had erected awe-inspiring temples, tombs, obelisks, and granite chapels. Unlike earlier pharaohs, she had restored old monuments

Like other pharaohs of the time, Hatshepsut erected many statues meant to depict her greatness for eternity.

Trying to sort out who lived when, how long each king ruled, and what happened on which dates in ancient Egypt is nearly impossible. Each time a new pharaoh took over, the Egyptians declared his first year of rule as year 1 in Egypt. If a pharaoh ruled for 22 years, for example, Egyptian calendars would begin with year 1 (the pharaoh's first year) and go to year 22. When the next pharaoh came to power, they would start with year 1 again. Egyptologists try their best to identify dates in terms of B.C. calendar years, but the years can't be determined with any certainty. Mostly, scientists rely on educated guesses and bits of evidence they have found to estimate the dates of each major era and the years each pharaoh reigned.

that had been destroyed by enemies or were crumbling away from age. Even today, Hatshepsut's own mortuary temple is considered one of the world's most magnificent structures. What remains of the temple's art and inscriptions has provided Egyptologists—people who study ancient Egypt—with much information about this ancient civilization.

Hatshepsut ordered the construction of hundreds of sculptures, mostly of herself. She organized successful missions to faraway lands and oversaw mining explorations. In addition, no civil wars occurred during her time as king.

Sometime after the pharaoh's death, mysterious events occurred. A massive campaign was mounted against her. Monuments were purposely damaged. Her kingly name was left off the lists of ruling kings. In many places where her royal name appeared, it had been scraped off the stone, and names of other closely related kings had been carved over it. Images of

her in carved reliefs and sculptures were viciously destroyed as well. The widespread destruction and defacement of her many works was clearly an attempt to bury all traces that she ever existed.

Another thing that may have shocked Egyptologists was discovering that Hatshepsut was not a male king. "He" was a "she"—a woman who had stepped up in a male-dominated society and ruled in a traditionally male fashion.

Hatshepsut, like every pharaoh, was considered a god. The pharaoh was thought to be the only human being able to communicate with the ancient Egyptian gods. He served as a link between the gods and the people under his rule. The pharaoh was also head of the government, the military, and the priesthood. All the land belonged to the pharaoh, and all the people labored for him.

The pharaohs built massive pyramids and underground tombs, where their mummies were to lie after death. They conquered in terrible wars, which they believed were won by the grace of the gods. They erected gigantic monuments to themselves, covering them with images and hieroglyphs detailing their mighty acts.

Because each generation felt the pressure to repeat or outdo the achievements of their ancestors, detailed records were kept, both in words and pictures. As more and more of these records came to light in modern times, it sparked a new form of study: Egyptology. By the mid-1800s, people journeyed to Egypt with hopes of uncovering a bit of Egypt's lost civilization and buried treasures. Most of these people were wealthy men from Western countries. But today Egyptologists, both men and women, come

Some early Egyptologists were more concerned with finding treasure than trying to reconstruct history.

from around the world, and Egyptology has become an archaeological science.

Every now and then, more ancient remains are discovered. New clues have been unveiled that fill in bits of history's gaps. Egyptologists have assembled a timeline of rulership dating back at least 5,000 years—even though the Egyptians didn't number their years the way we do today. Scientists have to estimate what year these were in historical time.

Egyptologists have identified several different periods in ancient Egyptian history. The names and dates given for these periods vary slightly among historians. Beginning with the earliest, they are generally known as the Predynastic period, the Early period, the Old Kingdom (or Pyramid Age), the First Intermediate period, the Middle Kingdom, the Second Intermediate period, the New Kingdom, the Third Intermediate period, and the Late period. Finally, there was the Greek period, which lasted from about 332 B.C. to 30 B.C. From then on, the Romans were in control of Egypt. This brought about the end of rule by the pharaohs —and the end of the ancient Egyptian civilization.

The major kingdoms, or eras, in which Egypt was a stable, prospering land are called the Old Kingdom (c. 2649–2100 B.C.), the Middle Kingdom (c. 2030–1650 B.C.), and the New Kingdom (c. 1550–1070 B.C.). The Old, Middle, and New kingdoms were times when several powerful pharaohs ruled one after the other, keeping the northern and southern halves of Egypt unified. During these times, the arts and culture of Egypt flourished.

Between these kingdoms were the intermediate periods—times of decline and chaos when more than one king ruled Egypt at a time. During these phases, the country was usually broken into various dynasties, all of them ruling at the same time and in control of separate regions. Although incomplete, long lists of the ruling pharaohs exist for these intermediate periods.

Hatshepsut was the New Kingdom's fifth ruler. Hatshepsut, meaning "foremost of noblewomen," was her given name, or nomen. Her pre-

nomen, or official throne name as pharaoh, was Maatkare. This name contained the word *maat*, meaning
"divine order." This was to assure her people that
she was rightfully pharaoh and that maat was fully
in place. Without her subjects' complete confidence,

*A relief from
one of Hatshep-
sut's temples
depicts the
pharaoh (right)
conducting a
ceremony with
Seshat, the god-
dess of writing
and knowledge.*

Hatshepsut's powers would have been questioned.

Since the 1920s, when major archaeological digs began to uncover more and more about her, Hatshepsut has been one of the most intriguing mysteries of this ancient world. How did she manage to become pharaoh, a feat that was unheard of for an Egyptian woman? Why did she choose to portray herself as a man, in regalia that only male kings wore? Who wanted to destroy all traces of her, and why?

For more than 100 years, Egyptologists around the world have been trying to piece Hatshepsut's life together. An amazing amount of factual details have come to light. What really happened, however, is still mostly a matter of theory and speculation. Of all the hidden secrets, some of the greatest lie with Hatshepsut.

The historical records discovered so far contain gaping holes that may never be filled. But they do prove one thing beyond a doubt: Famous Egyptian queens such as Nefertiti and Cleopatra VII pale in comparison with this early New Kingdom pharaoh.

In fact, Maatkare Hatshepsut, King of Upper and Lower Egypt, could easily be called the world's first powerful female ruler. But will her secrets ever be fully revealed? ♋

Chapter

2 DIVINE BIRTH

༺২৩৯

Although Hatshepsut held the title of King's Daughter at a young age, she was not born destined to rule a great nation. No woman in the ancient world was ever destined to rule alone. The exact year of her birth is unknown, but it was during one of the most prosperous periods of ancient Egypt. It may have been as early as 1490 B.C., and she might have been born in the city of Thebes (modern-day Luxor), on the eastern edge of the Nile River.

Hatshepsut's royal blood came from her mother, Ahmose, who was probably a sister or close relative of Amenhotep I, the New Kingdom's second ruler. Hatshepsut's father, Thutmose I, may have either been a distant royal relative or a non-royal who had an important position within the royal family. He appears to have been Amenhotep's vizier, or chief minister, the position closest in power to pharaoh. He could have been a military general as well.

Whatever his position, Thutmose proved himself to King Amenhotep. Before his death, Amenhotep I chose Thutmose I as his successor, probably because he didn't have a son of his own. As the third pharaoh of the New Kingdom, Thutmose I went on to become one of the greatest leaders of the era.

Surviving inscriptions indicate that he may not yet have been king at the time of Hatshepsut's birth. In any case, he and Ahmose would have strictly followed the customs of the culture. This included taking every precaution to ensure the safe birth of their child.

In ancient Egypt, giving birth meant facing many dangers. Complications could arise. Infant death was common, and mothers often did not survive childbirth. Everything possible was done to protect the mother and child.

This protection began before birth with the use of spells and

> *The hieroglyphic language of the ancient Egyptians does not include vowel sounds. Therefore, modern translators have to supply the vowels and can only guess at the proper spelling and pronunciations of names and other words. For this reason, every ancient Egyptian name can be found with multiple spellings, depending on the vowels each translator supplies. This adds to the confusion that already exists in the records. For example, the most powerful god in Egypt can be spelled Amen-Re, Amun-Re, or Amon-Ra.*

talismans, charms with supposedly magic powers. These were important parts of the rites of protection. The "birthing pavilion" where Hatshepsut would have been born was also designed to provide a luxurious, protective environment. The pavilion was often like a breezy tent set up in a garden or other serene place, which was important in the hot climate. Painted images of the hippopotamus goddess Tawaret and the dwarf god Bes decorated the pavilion walls or columns. Bes'

Bes was considered to be the protector of households, women, and children.

Because the infant death rate in ancient Egypt was high, talismans, charms, and magic spells were used in an attempt to prevent and cure childhood illnesses and ward off death. A spell for protection during pregnancy called for help from Hathor, the goddess of love and fertility. The words of the spell were said four times while the mother held an amulet showing Bes' image. When the mother went into labor, she placed the amulet against her forehead to help with delivery. Another remedy, meant to help a sick baby get well, was for the nursing mother to eat a mouse. Although some of the remedies seem extreme, the Egyptians were willing to try anything to heal a sick child, since no proven medicine was available.

hideous face and Tawaret's frightening hippopotamus form were meant to scare away evil spirits that might come to harm the mother or child.

At the time of Hatshepsut's birth, it is likely that close female friends, relatives, and servants gathered to help Ahmose. In the birthing pavilion, the women would have had privacy and quiet. Breezes from the Nile would have cooled the women as the mother labored, while Thutmose waited anxiously elsewhere in the palace.

At the moment of her baby's birth, Ahmose may have followed the ancient Egyptian custom of calling out the already chosen name of the newborn. The Egyptians believed that an infant did not really begin to exist until its name was uttered. After the birth, Hatshepsut's mother probably stayed in seclusion for two weeks, performed purification rituals, and kept her new baby close to her. When the 14 days had passed, she would again join the family and present her daughter publicly.

Hatshepsut's life began with her name spoken aloud. Her birth may have been ordinary, but later—as pharaoh—she claimed her birth was nothing less than divine.

Remarkably, a detailed account of this divine conception and birth has survived and appears on the walls of Hatshepsut's magnificent mortuary temple. It was dedicated to Amen-Re, the king of all the Egyptian gods and the god she called her father. Hatshepsut named the temple Djeser-Djeseru, or "holiest of the holies." It was excavated over several decades beginning in the mid-1800s and now stands as a breathtaking work of art and the crowning

Hatshepsut's temple, Djeser-Djeseru, has three terraces that reach 97 feet (29.6 meters) in height.

achievement of Hatshepsut's reign. The 3,000-year-old structure showed more creativity than any ancient Egyptian temple that came before it. Built of fine limestone, Djeser-Djeseru has a commanding presence even today. With its wide, stepped terraces and long walkways marked with magnificent columns, the elegant building is similar to the Greek designs that came centuries later.

Given the temple's original design, it's not surprising that Hatshepsut chose to build this temple at Deir el Bahri, a desert region west of the Nile. There an arc of jagged sandstone cliffs towers hundreds of feet above the barren ground. Cool-looking and pale at dawn, the cliff face glows a golden red in the setting sun, giving the land its own dramatic flair. Now uncovered and rebuilt by archaeologists, Djeser-Djeseru sits at the base of those cliffs like a white jewel in a giant pink shell.

The story of Hatshepsut's divine birth is painted on the walls of the north portico of the temple's second level. In one of the early hieroglyphs, Amen-Re makes an announcement to 12 lesser gods. He tells them he will father a child who will receive

The royal city of Thebes was the religious center of the Egyptian world and the site of Karnak, the enormous holy temple complex devoted primarily to Amen. In Hatshepsut's time, Amen was considered the creator of the universe and the most important of all the deities. Joined with the sun god, Re, he was worshipped as Amen-Re, the giver of all life.

"all lands and all countries." Amen-Re then takes the form of Hatshepsut's father, Thutmose I, and goes to Ahmose's rooms. As they sit together, he breathes life into Ahmose, and their child is conceived. Amen-Re tells her the child will be named Hatshepsut Khnemet-Amen, meaning "joined with Amen, Foremost of Noblewomen." He further declares that the child is destined to be king.

One of the final scenes shows the royal baby Hatshepsut being created on a potter's wheel by the ram-headed god, Khnum. Along with the baby's physical body, a similar form—known as the royal *ka*—is being fashioned at the same time. The ka was at the

The god Khnum molded an Egyptian child while the god Thoth measured the child's lifespan.

center of the ancient Egyptian belief system. The ka spirit gave life to the body and survived it after death. The royal ka contained the spirit of kingship.

The creation of the royal ka was of great importance to the Egyptian ruler. It proved that he—or in this case, she—was divinely chosen to rule the land. Khnum tells Amen-Re, "I will shape for thee thy daughter ... King of Upper and Lower Egypt." In these carvings, Hatshepsut's ka is clearly shown as male. It seems that Khnum could grant a person more than one ka if he felt like doing so. At Djeser-Djeseru, Hatshepsut claimed to have nine separate kas. Of these, eight were supposedly male.

The hieroglyphs go on to explain that when Hatshepsut was finally born, Amen-Re, her parents, and all the assembled gods and goddesses surrounded her and welcomed her with great love and joy. Amen-Re proclaimed that she was the next to be king. In these scenes, the infant is depicted as a boy. In other words, Hatshepsut claimed that her gender was flexible or changeable to her divine father, Amen-Re, even though the ancient Egyptians felt differently.

This detailed story on the walls of Djeser-Djeseru had an important purpose: Hatshepsut was proclaiming her divine birthright to be king. Without this connection to the gods, no pharaoh could last long. And for a female king coming to the throne in a way that no woman had before, it was even harder to gain the support of the Egyptian people. She needed to make a grand statement.

Other scenes at Djeser-Djeseru show Hatshepsut as a child being appointed co-ruler with Thutmose I—Hatshepsut's attempt to explain to her people that she was meant to rule as king even as a child. However, Egyptologists do not think this was the case. Although a member of the royal family, it is unlikely that she ever ruled alongside her father. She was a princess—not a prince. The role of king came to her gradually and only after the death of her father. ❧

3 A ROYAL CHILDHOOD

The royal lines of pharaonic families, called dynasties, can be traced back approximately 5,000 years. Within a dynasty, the title of pharaoh was passed down through the men of a single family or bloodline. When there was no male relative to inherit the throne, an unrelated ruler would take over. This would usually mark the beginning of a new dynasty. The 18th dynasty—the dynasty Hatshepsut was born into—began in a dramatic way.

In the ancient world, before the time of the pharaohs, invaders from many regions had fought to win control of the Nile Valley. In the time just before the mid-1500s B.C., foreign invaders known as the Hyksos had control of much of Egypt. It was a divided land, with the pharaonic dynasties holding power mostly

A pharaoh was adorned with the crowns of Upper and Lower Egypt, symbolizing his rule over both parts of the unified country.

29

The Hyksos introduced the horse-drawn chariot and new weapons into Egypt.

in Upper Egypt, which was the southern part of the Nile Valley. But around 1550 B.C., an Egyptian pharaoh managed to drive out the Hyksos. Rid of the enemy, Upper and Lower Egypt were finally a unified nation once more. The pharaoh who accomplished this feat was named Ahmose, like Hatshepsut's mother. Ahmose's victory made him one of the most powerful pharaohs ever to rule Egypt.

The ancient Egyptians were cautious and conservative people. They did not want to live in unsettled times and were superstitious about change. They believed that change destroyed maat, or the divine order of things. To have more than one ruler at a time was against maat as well. In the eyes of the people, Ahmose's victory restored peace and prosperity after decades of civil war and chaos.

This also signaled the beginning of the New Kingdom and the founding of the 18th dynasty. The New Kingdom, which lasted more than 400 years, was a high point in ancient Egyptian civilization. Much of the glory of that time was due to the accomplishments of Hatshepsut once she became pharaoh. Although it is difficult to know for sure, she was likely King Ahmose's great-granddaughter. Ahmose fathered the second 18th dynasty ruler, Amenhotep I, who in turn was followed by Thutmose I, Hatshepsut's father.

Upon his coronation in about 1504 B.C., Thutmose I was considered a royal and divine being. It was crucial to keep the power within his own family. For royal ruling families, maintaining power meant keeping the royal blood "pure." To accomplish this, a new pharaoh often married someone from his own family rather than an "outsider" who had no royal ties. Brothers often married sisters or half-sisters. The 18th dynasty had begun with a full brother-sister marriage. Pharaohs sometimes married their own daughters if there were no relatives more suitable or if the leading queen was considered too old. Among the ruling class in ancient Egypt, this was considered normal and expected. The common people, however, shunned this practice.

From the time she was a child, Hatshepsut was undoubtedly aware of her family's heritage, but she probably never imagined that she would be king of Egypt someday. She was a little princess, and her mother was the highest-ranking wife of a divine king. As such, Ahmose had the primary royal title of

The columns in the temples of Amen displayed great tales of Egypt's history.

God's Wife, meaning that she was a priestess who performed sacred rituals in the temples of Amen. Hatshepsut's heritage put her at the highest level of society, but she was still a woman. Her high standing did not mean that she could take the throne of Egypt.

Once her father became pharaoh, Hatshepsut and her mother would have lived in their own private residence. This luxurious home was part of the pharaoh's palace complex but separate from the royal harem—a palace building where other female members of the royal family lived with their children, both girls and very young boys. Residents of the harem included wives and children of noblemen working for the pharaoh, female relatives of earlier Egyptian kings, nurses, and other female members of the staff. Egyptian kings often took several lesser wives who lived in the harem, too. It was necessary that the king have as many children as possible so he could maintain the family line.

In the harem nursery, the young

The word queen *did not exist in the ancient Egyptian language. Rather, a woman in this position was called "king's wife." The chief royal wife often held the title of God's Wife of Amen, the most powerful priestess in all of Egypt. The Great Royal Wife was a crucial role because society dictated that a pharaoh could not rule alone. To uphold both maat and religious tradition, a wife was necessary. This female counterpart played a role in the divine order that the pharaoh could not. By performing the ritual duties and religious ceremonies expected of her, she helped keep the kingdom's affairs balanced and orderly.*

The royal family's residence was called the Per'ao, or "great house." From this Egyptian word comes the English word pharaoh. The pharaoh's Great House would have been huge, elaborate, and luxurious. These palaces were hidden behind walls and had flat roofs where families could sit and enjoy cooler air. Royal families had beautiful furniture made of exotic wood. Their homes included gardens, pools, shade trees, and flowers such as lotus blossoms. Few of these structures exist today. Most were made of mud brick or other materials that did not hold up over time. The only buildings the pharaohs were concerned with preserving were their temples and tombs, which needed to last for eternity.

Hatshepsut played with other children. When the children were about 4 years old, the playful days of childhood came to an end and the children's education began. Children of the harem and of important court officials were taught by a Teacher of Royal Children. Education was usually reserved for boys, but girls of a higher social status probably went to school, too. It is almost certain that Hatshepsut received the best education available as she grew up in the royal palace.

None of Thutmose I's monuments mentions his daughter Hatshepsut. All that is known of her childhood or her early years in the royal court comes from inscriptions and pictures found on temples and monuments erected by Hatshepsut herself when she was king. These records were created only after she was pharaoh. None of them describe the simple details of her everyday activities as a young girl.

Some artwork and inscriptions on a small temple connected to

Djeser-Djeseru depict Hatshepsut as a boy dressed in pharaoh's clothing and sitting on the lap of the great god Amen. Every temple scene she created was meant to establish her right to be king.

Other paintings and inscriptions there tell the story of her travels throughout Egypt as a young girl with her father. According to these scenes, Thutmose introduced his daughter to much of the land she would one day rule. They visited the Hathor temple in their home city of Thebes. On the island of Elephantine, they spent time at the temple of the god Khnum. Thutmose also probably took Hatshepsut to see the great pyramids of Giza and Cheops, monuments that were already 1,000 years old when she was born.

There are 10 pyramids in Giza, including the three largest and best-preserved pyramids in Egypt.

The two are also said to have traveled to the city of Heliopolis in the far north, where Hatshepsut supposedly experienced her coronation as co-ruler with her father.

In many ways, Hatshepsut probably had a typical childhood, or at least a typical royal childhood. In the hot, sunny climate of Egypt, young children rarely wore clothing. Their heads were most likely shaved except for a long piece of hair that hung down from the side of the head. Egyptian children wore this traditional style, called the "sidelock of youth," until they began to mature.

Egyptian girls played with dolls, wooden toys, and games of all kinds. Being part of a royal family, Hatshepsut had the best of everything, including all the luxuries a palace could offer. Such a palace usually included a zoo filled with exotic animals. To fill these zoos, leopards, monkeys, baboons, crocodiles, and many other creatures were brought to Thebes from surrounding lands.

Hatshepsut grew up as the only child of the royal couple. The pharaoh and the Great Royal Wife were expected to have as many children as possible. Sons and daughters who could marry one another would ensure that rulership continued to pass down through the royal family. But apparently Ahmose did not give birth to sons. Before Hatshepsut, another daughter was born and named Nefrubiti (also known as

Achbetneferu). But this child died sometime before the age of 5.

Thutmose I did have sons, but these were most likely the children of lesser wives. Two of the sons, Wadjmose and Amenmose, appear in the ancient records but probably did not live beyond their teenage years. A third possible son—Rekmose— is occasionally mentioned, too. No one knows the mysterious ends of these three young princes. But one of Thutmose I's sons did survive him. He was the child of Mutnofret, and they named him Thutmose II.

As the two surviving children of the pharaoh Thutmose I, Hatshepsut and Thutmose II had a clear destiny before them. It did not matter who was the elder, and it made no difference whether they felt any romantic attraction. Given their place in society, they would be expected to marry and carry their family's dynasty forward as king and Great Royal Wife. Hatshepsut was also to become the great priestess, the God's Wife of Amen. ❧

Trying to understand how family members in ancient Egypt were related is nearly impossible. Almost all the clues come from the titles and their names in inscriptions or from paintings that show them in certain family connections. Beyond the immediate family, the ancient Egyptians did not have specific names for relationships, such as uncle or grandmother. Egyptologists disagree on who the mother of Hatshepsut's brothers Amenmose and Wadjmose was. Some claim she was a minor wife, possibly also Mutnofret. There is strong evidence that she was at least the mother of Wadjmose. But other experts state that both were sons of Ahmose.

4 THE GOD'S WIFE

❧❀❧

In about 1492 B.C., Thutmose I "rested from life, going forth to heaven, having completed his years in gladness of heart." During his reign, Thutmose had been a great warrior who kept Egypt's enemies from regaining control of the throne. He conquered new lands and undertook many important building projects. All of this had increased both Egypt's power and the power of the pharaoh. With Thutmose's death, the next pharaoh would be expected to do the same.

Although Thutmose II was the only male heir, he was still the son of a lesser wife. To boost his claim to the throne, he married his half-sister Hatshepsut. Still, Thutmose II could not be crowned king until his father was buried. As the incoming rulers, Hatshepsut and Thutmose II made sure that Thutmose I's

A pharaoh would visit the construction sites of his monuments and building projects to make sure they were going as planned.

During mummification, the body was packed with natron, a salty substance that caused tissues to dry out, preventing decay. The brain, thought to be useless after death, was pulled out through the nose with a hook and thrown away. A long cut was made in the side of the body to remove other major organs. The heart was left in the body, but the lungs, liver, intestines, and stomach were removed. Each was washed, dried, and preserved with natron in its own container. The body was then wrapped in linen cloth and placed in its coffin.

body was carefully prepared for the afterlife by the process of mummification. The funeral rites were then performed and the king's body was placed in a tomb.

Thutmose had selected a remote spot for his tomb in a desert valley west of Deir el Bahri. He was the first pharaoh to be buried there. After him, many pharaohs dug their tombs at the necropolis—or cemetery—known today as the Valley of the Kings.

No one knows for sure whether Hatshepsut and Thutmose II were married when their father died. But at the time of their marriage, neither of them was an adult. Hatshepsut was probably between 12 and 15, and Thutmose was probably a few years older or younger.

Hatshepsut took the traditional vows to be "feminine to a divine degree, to exude fragrance as she walked, and speak in tones that filled the palace with music." The most important vow was "to make herself loved," and to do so, she pledged to "tend her lord with love and affection."

In her life as an unmarried royal princess, Hatshepsut had held the simple title of King's Daughter. But with her brother-husband's coronation, she took on the important role of King's Great Royal Wife. She also held the titles of God's Wife of Amen and King's Sister.

More than 60 tombs of Egyptian rulers from the New Kingdom are in the Valley of the Kings.

As king, Thutmose II carried on his father's tradition as best he could. Historians believe he was a frail and possibly sickly man. He was successful at some minor military operations, but compared with his father's great achievements, Thutmose II's military successes were insignificant. It is possible, however, that the records of his battles have been lost.

It seems to have been a time of peace, and Thutmose apparently put his efforts into other things besides warfare. He directed the building of monuments and other works. These included adding to the huge temple complex at Karnak on the east side of the Nile in Egypt's southern capital of Thebes.

Thutmose's ancient monuments indicate that Hatshepsut performed her royal wifely duties as a humble King's Wife. In many works depicting her with Thutmose, she appears in a secondary position, as a proper wife and queen would. She is usually dressed in a long, fitted sheath and a crown. Where her mother

Many pharaohs continued to add to the impressive Karnak temple, which was dedicated to the god Amen-Re. Hieroglyphs on the magnificent columns detailed their accomplishments.

appears, Hatshepsut is portrayed standing behind both her mother and her husband, as was the tradition.

She also fulfilled her role as mother. During the New Kingdom, royal daughters were many and surviving royal sons were few. Hatshepsut gave birth to a daughter, but as far as history reveals, she and Thutmose had no sons. Whether they had a second daugher is another unanswered question. With infant mortality so high, it is possible that Hatshepsut bore another daughter who did not live to see adulthood.

Hatshepsut's one daughter on record was named Neferure. However, at least two inscriptions left by men who tutored Neferure have suggested there was another, younger daughter named Meritre. One of Neferure's tutors claims to have educated "the elder daughter, the royal daughter" Neferure when she was a child. Another royal tutor was Senenmut, who took a role of major importance during Hatshepsut's kingship. He wrote, "I fed the eldest daughter of the king," or, in another translation, "the eldest royal daughter." If no daughters existed besides Neferure, why would these men have referred to her as the eldest?

Additionally, the name Meritre-Hatshepsut—called Hatshepsut II by some historians—was also discovered. This girl was younger than Hatshepsut, and some believe she could have been her second daughter. But nowhere on Hatshepsut's own monuments does she mention the name Meritre-Hatshepsut.

Most Egyptologists claim the similarity between their names is a coincidence.

Neferure was a beloved child, and not just by her parents. Senenmut had been brought in by Hatshepsut to be her daughter's guardian and tutor. Senenmut was of humble birth, but he could read and write. He had begun his career as a military scribe, and over many years, he became Hatshepsut's most trusted official.

With Senenmut entrusted with the care of

Many of Senenmut's statues depict the close and protective role he had in Neferure's life.

Neferure, Hatshepsut was able to turn her attention to another important task. She wanted to construct a lavish tomb where she could eventually hide her mummy from tomb robbers and ensure her safe journey to the afterlife. There she would accompany her husband, the king.

In ancient Egypt, the rituals of preparation for death were highly complex and taken seriously. It was crucial that the body be preserved. Without it, the ka—or soul—could not journey to the land of the gods. If the body was destroyed, the ka would experience what was known as the "second death." The possibility of this fate filled every Egyptian with horror. This is why Egyptians buried their dead rather than burned the bodies. This is also why they invented the practice of mummification, for those who could afford it.

Hatshepsut chose an isolated location for her queen's tomb, but she ended up never occupying it. Events were about to change Hatshepsut's position in the royal family and the course of her life. ❧

Senenmut quickly became a trusted official in the royal court—beginning with either Thutmose I or Thutmose II. He was clearly Hatshepsut's favorite of all those working for her. Senenmut held as many as 80 titles—the highest being Chief Steward of Amen, awarded to him by Hatshepsut. Senenmut's list of accomplishments is exceptional. One of the most important was his involvement in the building of Hatshepsut's mortuary temple. Although he is never named as its architect, he played a major role in its construction.

5 STEPS TO THE THRONE

❧⚬❧

Some early Egyptologists believed Hatshepsut was scheming to become king while she was married. They thought she was stronger than Thutmose II and was a power-hungry woman. But there is no evidence that Hatshepsut was dissatisfied with her role as the Great Royal Wife and God's Wife of Amen. It may be impossible to prove that she expected to be anything more.

But sometime around 1479 B.C., Thutmose II died, leaving the throne empty after a reign of three to 15 years. Most Egyptologists believe Thutmose II was probably a sick or physically weak man. When his mummy was discovered, its skin was pitted and pockmarked, showing that he probably died of disease—perhaps smallpox. The unfinished state of his tomb suggests that his death was unexpected.

Many statues of Hatshepsut mixed her femininity with pharaonic symbols, such as the pharaoh's false beard and headdress.

The king was gone, but his wife—the high priestess and the God's Wife of Amen—remained. Who would inherit the throne? Hatshepsut had more royal blood and experience than any other candidate. She was a King's Daughter, a King's Sister, and a King's Wife. But she was not a man, and she had likely failed to give birth to any sons.

Thutmose II did have a son who should have been the obvious choice. But that son, Thutmose III, was the child of a secondary wife. His mother, Isis, had no royal blood. Also, Thutmose III was only a child—maybe even a baby—when his father died. He was not old enough to take charge of a country. He needed a regent—someone to rule on his behalf until he was old enough to become pharaoh himself. No one was more qualified than Hatshepsut, and she stepped up to the job immediately.

Isis was a lesser wife, which jeopardized Thutmose III's chances of becoming pharaoh.

Inscriptions found in the tomb of Ineni, an architect who served the Thutmose dynasty, spell out the situation:

[Thutmose II's] son stood in his place as King of the Two Lands, having assumed the rulership upon the throne of the one who begat [produced] him, while his [Thutmose II's] sister, the God's Wife, Hatshepsut, managed the affairs of the country, the Two Lands being in her care.

The name of Thutmose III is not even mentioned in the inscription. Ineni makes it clear that Hatshepsut was at the head of the government by naming her specifically. But for her to become regent was probably all that was expected.

Other Egyptian queens before her had watched over the affairs of the country when necessary. Like Hatshepsut, some of these royal women had become regents for sons who inherited the throne as children. Others ruled while their husbands or sons were away at war or for other reasons. But ancient records show only traces of evidence that any woman before Hatshepsut held the official title of pharaoh.

As regent, Hatshepsut wasted no time making sure Thutmose III was recognized as king, even though he was only a child. It was crucial that the leadership of Egypt remain within her family.

Thutmose was too young to marry, as was Hatshepsut's daughter Neferure, the likely candidate for a wife who could ensure his kingship through a proper bloodline. Lacking a royal mother, he had less of a right to rule. Such a weak position might have led men outside the family to steal the title of pharaoh.

By proclaiming Thutmose III as pharaoh, Hatshepsut was ensuring that people would see her nephew-stepson as the true ruler. A temple inscription from the second year of Thutmose III's reign states that he was "sole King of Upper and Lower Egypt and the Lord of the Two Lands." With this inscription, he is depicted receiving the white crown of the pharaoh. His royal cartouche also indicates he was considered king.

Ancient Egyptian rulers followed the custom of inscribing their names within an oval-shaped cartouche to signify their power as sons of Re. The border of the cartouche, meant to look like a rope, symbolized eternity, or everlasting life. Within the cartouche, the king's throne name would usually appear in hieroglyphs, followed by his—or her—personal name.

Before Hatshepsut, several women had ruled Egypt. Three prominent ones were Nitocris, Sobeknofrure, and Tetisheri. During the 17th and 18th dynasties, women began to be accepted in important political roles. Tetisheri was the grandmother of Ahmose, first pharaoh of the New Kingdom and probably related to Hatshepsut. Records reveal that these female rulers controlled Egypt for only short periods, just as the ruling family's royal line was dying out. This makes Hatshepsut unique. She ruled for a long period during a golden age. She was also the first and only female ruler to have herself portrayed as a man.

Hieroglyphs from a sacred chamber depict three of Thutmose III's names. The first line shows his god's name, "Mighty Bull, Arising in Thebes." The second and third lines show cartouches of his prenomen (throne name) and nomen (birth name).

As she had with her husband, Hatshepsut kept to the traditional role expected of her. In other monuments from the earliest years of Thutmose III's reign, she is again shown standing behind the new king. The king, though still a child, is depicted as an adult. Also, even a boy ruler needed someone to fill the female role, and so Hatshepsut continued with these duties as the great priestess, the God's Wife of Amen. Doing so probably kept the Amen-Re temple priests on her side.

Because Thutmose III was a baby, his title of king was merely symbolic. But it seems that at least in the first few years of his reign, Hatshepsut made no attempts to be viewed as pharaoh herself. Still, she did not hide the fact that she had full authority in making decisions for the country.

As the months passed, Hatshepsut must have considered what her role was and what it could become. At that point, Thutmose had no say in the government, but as he grew older, he would be expected to take over. Members of the court who might not agree to a co-regency, or joint rule, could put pressure on Thutmose to make Hatshepsut step down and let him rule alone. Or if Thutmose died early—as many infants did—the power would again be up for grabs. By proclaiming herself pharaoh, Hatshepsut could keep such things from happening and keep the rule of Egypt within the family dynasty. Rule of the Two Lands would then remain fully in her own hands.

No record remains of Hatshepsut's coronation as king, if such an event ever took place. Many experts say there had to have been a point at which she was officially crowned king, since this is how she would have achieved her divine status. Others believe she just gradually slipped more and more into this powerful role. It is unlikely that anyone will ever know for sure. But by Thutmose III's seventh regnal year—his seventh year as king—things had changed.

By year 7, official seals bearing Hatshepsut's royal cartouche existed. There were also grave goods found marked with her royal throne names that date to year 7 of Thutmose III's reign. Their inscriptions refer to her as "the Great Goddess Maatkare." Egyptologists consider this proof that by this year, Hatshepsut had become the acknowledged ruler of all Egypt. ✑

6 TRANSFORMATION

❧❧❧

Inscriptions found on ancient monuments and on stone pillars or slabs called stelae detail the dramatic transformation Hatshepsut made from God's Wife to pharaoh. Over time, her image evolved from distinctly feminine to fully masculine, displaying all the symbols of a royal male ruler.

Early scenes of Hatshepsut dressed in female attire gave way to images of mixed gender. In a block from the Chapelle Rouge ("red chapel") at Karnak, she is dressed as a woman, but she is also wearing a crown with feathers and ram's horns, which only a male king would wear. An inscription described her as the King of Upper and Lower Egypt and is followed by Hatshepsut's royal cartouche.

In other art, Hatshepsut is wearing a woman's

Hieroglyphs at Hatshepsut's temple show her in masculine form, offering gifts to the god Horus.

55

ankle-length dress while striding forward in long steps. Before her time, paintings and carvings always showed women with their feet together. Only men were depicted with any sense of movement.

Hatshepsut's monuments at her morturary temple in Deir el Bahri also depict her in a pharaoh's regalia. First she is seen wearing a short linen royal skirt that was part of a king's attire. Later she added more of the traditional pharaoh's costume. This included the striped royal *nemes* headdress, the crook, the short-handled tool called a flail, and the wide circular collar called a pectoral. A heavy double crown signified the union of Upper and Lower Egypt, and it was always adorned with a uraeus—a cobra that was the ultimate symbol of pharaonic power. Hatshepsut is even depicted wearing the symbolic golden false beard of a pharaoh.

The images of Hatshepsut's body shifted as well. In earlier monuments, her physical form appears rounded and girlish. By the time she wears the pharaoh's regalia, she is portrayed as masculine, with broader shoulders and a flatter, more powerful body. This does not mean that her body changed, but that her depiction changed to fit her new role as king.

It is possible that Egypt's earlier female rulers may have thought of themselves as pharaohs, but none portrayed themselves as such. Hatshepsut's desire to appear male was probably because she was breaking tradition by calling herself a pharaoh. To

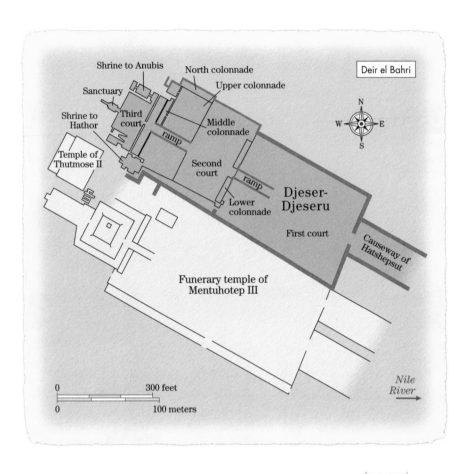

Shrine to Anubis
North colonnade
Upper colonnade
Sanctuary
Deir el Bahri
Shrine to Hathor
Third court
Middle colonnade
Temple of Thutmose II
Second court
Lower colonnade
First court
Djeser-Djeseru
Causeway of Hatshepsut
Funerary temple of Mentuhotep III
Nile River

N W E S

0   300 feet
0   100 meters

ensure that she was given the status of a male ruler, she would need to be portrayed as a male pharaoh.

Hatshepsut made no attempts to pretend she was a man. She was surrounded by a group of men from the elite class who must have known she was a woman. They alone would have been able to move against her in any significant way. Instead, they left behind glowing testimonies of her.

Even as king, Hatshepsut did not forget certain

In regnal year 7, Hatshepsut appointed Senenmut to oversee the construction of her mortuary temple. Senenmut also may have been in charge of designing the magnificent structure.

Hatshepsut was eventually depicted strictly as a man in pharaoh's regalia doing masculine activities, such as running.

aspects of femininity. Archaeologists have found objects—such as jewelry and carved alabaster pots that typically held eye makeup—that bear her royal cartouche. In one inscription, she refers to herself as "more beautiful than anything."

Despite Hatshepsut's appearance, inscriptions continued to use both "he" and "she" or "him" and "her," sometimes within a single sentence. Although she adopted nearly all the usual titles of a pharaoh, there was one she never used: the extremely masculine pharaonic title of Mighty Bull.

Hatshepsut had no surviving male family members to advise or protect her and her young nephew-stepson. Therefore, she wanted to prove that her position as king was valid so that she could continue the family bloodline. One way was to show herself chosen as a child by Thutmose I to rule alongside him. Another was claiming to be the daughter of Amen-Re through divine birth.

If Hatshepsut had an official coronation, she should have marked the year it occurred as her first year of rule. But on later monuments, she claims she became pharaoh at the same time Thutmose III did, meaning their joint reign was a co-regency. She did this even though earlier monuments show that she was not recognized as king at first.

Nevertheless, Hatshepsut was making a clear statement: Although she was female, she had the power and attributes necessary to rule and be respected as a male king. If she could rule until Thutmose III came of age and had children of his own, the family lineage would be safe.

Rather than referring to herself as a Mighty Bull, Hatshepsut related to a feminine deity. She worshipped Hathor, the goddess of love and fertility. She built a private Hathor chapel on one side of Djeser-Djeseru. Scenes at Deir el Bahri show Hatshepsut being nursed by Hathor, whom she called her mother. Hathor was often portrayed in the form of a cow, with long horns that held the sun between them. Hathor also appeared as a beautiful young woman with cow's ears. Other times, she is shown as a woman with a cow's head.

7 MONUMENTAL ACHIEVEMENTS

❧❦❧

Egypt in the 18th dynasty was growing like never before. It was a vast and powerful kingdom, with most of the Middle East under its control. The Hyksos were gone, and the country's boundaries stretched far in both southern and eastern directions. This was the all-powerful kingdom that Hatshepsut took control of. She had successfully made the transition to pharaoh, inheriting the powers, privileges, and burdens that came with the title. But she could not have done so without the support of her inner circle.

Many Egyptologists of the 1900s were convinced that a woman could not have capably ruled Egypt. They theorized that Hatshepsut was a puppet for the men behind her. Some even believed that Senenmut was running things while keeping Hatshepsut distracted. But her many achievements and her supporters' devotion to her—as shown in their own personal inscriptions—prove otherwise.

In a wise political move, Hatshepsut surrounded herself with loyal administrators with both political and religious backgrounds. Historically, these two groups tended to be at odds. This could spell disaster for a pharaoh if one side was with him and the other side was trying to bring him down. Having strong supporters on both sides protected him against betrayal.

Hatshepsut came to power at a time when Egypt was flourishing and its boundaries were growing.

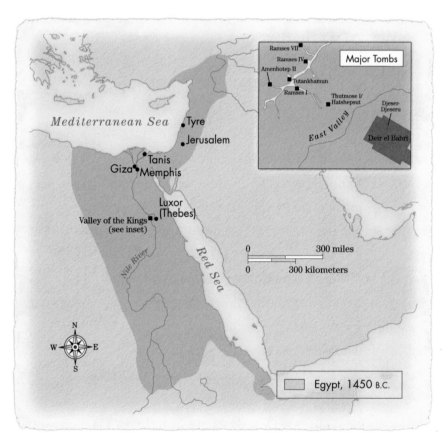

Of these, Senenmut was held in the highest esteem. One of his many inscriptions reads, "He [Hatshepsut] … appointed me to be chief of his estate … I was superior of superiors, the chief of chiefs of works." In other inscriptions, Senenmut describes his more personal connection to Hatshepsut: "I was the real favorite of the king, acting as one praised by his lord every day." Another inscription read, "I was one whose steps were known in the palace, a real confidant of the King, his beloved: Overseer of the Garden of Amen, Senenmut."

While Thutmose III was young, the only person with more power than Senenmut was Hatshepsut herself. But she relied heavily on at least two others in key positions. One of these, Hapuseneb, was head of the priesthood and the "chief of prophets North and South." He was also one of her leading architects and held the additional title of vizier of Upper Egypt.

Hapuseneb's support and approval of Hatshepsut was probably due to her supposed acceptance by the gods. With her rise to the throne, maat had not been disrupted. In fact, the nation was prospering and she was not being challenged in any way. Elites approved of her rule because it kept them prosperous. It also left them with the same privileges they had had at the death of Thutmose II. Few would have dared to contest her rights when she was so visibly favored by the gods and had the support of so many elite families.

Another trusted adviser was Hatshepsut's treasurer, Thuty, who oversaw her vast fortune. He was also a skilled craftsman who decorated many of Hatshepsut's temples using metal, precious stones, and costly woods.

Her administrators were in place, but the pharaoh needed a Great Royal Wife. Because Hatshepsut was a woman, the Great Royal Wife would not literally be a wife, but simply an appropriate woman to fulfill the role and perform rituals. For this important job, Hatshepsut chose her daughter, Neferure.

It was probably assumed that, given their positions in the royal family, Neferure and Thutmose III would someday marry. So Hatshepsut may have selected Neferure to fill the role of the God's Wife of Amen as a way to begin training her for marriage. But some historians suspect that Hatshepsut may have been positioning Neferure to inherit the throne herself. They wonder whether she was attempting to establish a tradition of female rulers. One small clue that this was the case is found in one of the many statues of Neferure with Senenmut.

In one depiction, Hatshepsut appears with Thuty, helping to weigh the heaps of gold, silver, and myrrh that were hers. It also indicates the pride and satisfaction Hatshepsut felt as an accomplished ruler: "She [Hatshepsut] exhaled the odors of the divine dew, her fragrance reached as far as [the distant land of] Punt, it mingled with the odors of Punt. Her skin was like kneaded gold and her face shone like stars."

In one statue, the child Neferure is wearing a pharaoh's false beard.

In any case, neither of these two possibilities ever played out. In regnal year 11, all mention of Neferure mysteriously ends. This convinced historians that she must have died at this point or shortly thereafter.

There are at least 10 statues depicting both Senenmut and Neferure, but only one shows Hatshepsut's daughter with the false beard of a pharaoh.

But Hatshepsut's reign went on, and its achievements became more magnificent. Surrounded by master builders, she soon embarked on an ambitious monument-building program. Such building projects were meant to show how fully the gods had accepted her as king and to proclaim her close relationship with them—something that was only possible with a king.

The construction projects were widespread throughout Egypt, but her most spectacular works that have survived were centered on Thebes and dedicated to Amen. Hatshepsut never forgot to pay homage to her divine father, who she believed was always guiding her.

One of the most amazing of Hatshepsut's projects—aside from her mortuary temple at Deir el Bahri—was the construction of four gigantic obelisks at Karnak. These huge blocks of granite were taken from quarries in Aswan, south of Thebes. The obelisks were carved in Aswan and then transported north to be erected in the holy Karnak temple complex. The first pair of these colossal granite objects was completed early in her reign and dedicated to her late husband, Thutmose II.

The second pair is the most remarkable, and its creation was a tremendous undertaking. Carved from the quarry granite in Hatshepsut's 16th year as pharaoh, the huge objects were completed in only seven months. From the Aswan quarries, they were shipped miles away to Thebes on enormous barges, each propelled by 850 oarsmen. Once they arrived at Karnak, the obelisks stood so tall that the ceiling of the temple had to be dismantled just to accommodate them.

With the successful arrival of the obelisks in Karnak, a public celebration began. Hatshepsut and her priests performed ceremonial rituals. Offerings were made to the gods, including a slaughtered bull. Through this ceremony, the king officially dedicated the obelisks to her father, the great god Amen.

The tips of the obelisks were pyramid-shaped and covered in a combination of silver and gold. This gave them a blinding brilliance under the blazing Egyptian sun. Hatshepsut's royal titles were carved into their tips, and the columns of hieroglyphs carved on their sides described their construction and transport to the temple, as well as other events.

In ancient Egypt, obelisks were considered to be the embodiment of the living sun god. They had individual names, and the priests and rulers made offerings to them as if the god inhabited them. These New Kingdom objects weighed as much as 450 tons (405 metric tons) and stood about 100 feet (30.5 m) high. One giant obelisk found at the quarry site, possibly being created for Hatshepsut, cracked and was never transported to Thebes. Its measurements were far greater than the other obelisks. It weighed about 1,000 tons (900 metric tons) and, if erected, would have towered more than 134 feet (41 m). Since it is not inscribed, this obelisk may have belonged to later kings, such as Amenhotep III or Ramses II.

Three of these massive monuments eventually fell or were destroyed. The bases of the first two still sit beside a lake at Karnak. But the fourth obelisk, part of the second pair and weighing 323 tons (291 metric tons), still stands. At almost 97 feet (29.6 m), it remains Egypt's tallest standing obelisk.

Another one of Hatshepsut's many newly built structures was a monumental gateway at Karnak. Another huge undertaking, the gateway is known as

The hieroglyphs on Hatshepsut's obelisk include praises of the gods Horus and Amen-Re. They also detail Hatshepsut's divinity and rule.

the eighth pylon and was probably the main entrance to the temple complex during her reign.

Hatshepsut documented her restoration of many temples that were falling apart or were no longer used. Some of these restorations were of buildings that the Hyksos invaders had ruined. As usual with any Egyptian king, Hatshepsut was not shy about proclaiming these further achievements. At a shrine on the east bank of the Nile known as Speos Artemides, she had these words inscribed:

> *Hear ye, all people and folk as many as they may be, I have done these things through the counsel of my heart. I have not slept forgetfully, (but) I have restored that which had been ruined. I have raised up that which had gone to pieces formerly, since the Asiatics [Hyksos] were in the midst of Avaris of the Northland, and vagabonds were in the midst of them, overthrowing that which had been made.*

An inscription on one of Hatshepsut's monuments proclaims:

> I have made this with a loving heart for my father, Amen ... I have not been forgetful of any project he has decreed. ... [I know] that he is divine, and I have done it by his command. He is the one who guides me. ... I could not have imagined the work without his acting. ... My heart is perceptive on behalf of my father and I have access to his mind's knowledge ... for I know that Karnak is heaven on earth.

Hatshepsut was looking to the future so her name and works would endure forever.

8 THE MYSTERIOUS LAND OF PUNT

ᘓᗡᘚᗢᘓ

Besides building colossal monuments to glorify Amen-Re, Hatshepsut believed that the god was directing her to mount exploratory missions beyond the country. One of the grandest of these was the voyage in about 1475 B.C. to Punt, a mysterious land located somewhere near the southern banks of the Red Sea on the East African coast.

The purpose of the mission—which was organized by Senenmut and others, and led by Hatshepsut's chancellor, Neshi—was exploration and trade. Getting to Punt was difficult. The travelers first had to trek east from Thebes across miles of scorching desert sands. Upon reaching the banks of the Red Sea, they built and launched at least five Phoenician-style ships and sailed south to find Punt.

Paintings on Hatshepsut's temple display Egyptian soldiers with battle axes and palm fronds during the expedition to Punt.

This fabled place was also known as the "Terrace of Incense" and "God's Land" because of its fabulous treasures. The men's mission was to bring back valuable goods for use in Hatshepsut's mortuary temple and as offerings to Amen. The most important of these were the precious resins—frankincense and myrrh—available in Punt. The Egyptians needed these resins to make incense, a crucial ingredient in ritual offerings to the gods. Massive quantities of incense were burned daily in the temples of Hatshepsut's kingdom.

Arriving successfully in Punt, the men were greeted by Parotiu, the native chief. With him were his two sons, his daughter, and his wife, Ati, riding a small donkey. Punt was unlike anything the Egyptians had previously seen. The homes were round, thatch-roofed huts that stood above the marshy water on stilts. The men grew long beards that they braided in styles like the Egyptian gods. Everywhere the men saw wild animals, palm trees, and other exotic plants.

Trade between the people of Punt and the Egyptians went effortlessly. The cargo-laden ships that returned to Thebes carried many kinds of exotic treasure, which ancient records describe:

> *The loading of the ships very heavily with marvels of the country of Punt; all goodly fragrant woods of the God's Land, heaps of myrrh-resin, with fresh myrrh trees, with ebony and pure ivory, with green gold of Emu, with cinnamon wood, khesyt wood, with two kinds of incense, eye cosmetic, with apes, monkeys, dogs, and the skins of the southern panther, with natives and their children. Never was brought the like of this for any king who has been since the beginning.*

The Egyptians loaded several ships with goods and treasures from Punt.

Many other riches were brought back to Egypt, including live panthers, a cheetah, and a giraffe. For Hatshepsut, perhaps the greatest treasures were 31 incense trees. She planted them in a beautiful garden at her mortuary temple. Archaeologists have found the native soil of Punt still clinging to the rootballs of some of these trees.

The excursion to Punt was Hatshepsut's grandest mission outside Egypt, but it was not her only one. She set up mining operations in the Sinai to bring home turquoise and copper. Before setting up trade with Punt, she established a crucial trading mission with Phoenicia. The people of Phoenicia supplied wood and the expertise for building the ships that took the Egyptians on their voyage down the Red Sea.

Weapons, jewelry, jugs, and vases were some of the items brought back to Egypt from Punt.

There are also some hints that she may have waged war. When Hatshepsut ruled, few neighboring enemies would have gone against the mighty Egyptian forces. This may be why she left little mention of military action during her reign. Nevertheless, there is evidence that she may have carried out a few defensive military campaigns.

Hatshepsut continued to prove throughout her reign that her "masculine" actions made her an unconventional female king. After the voyage to Punt, she no longer needed to worry about being seen as a legitimate ruler. She was a pharaoh who brought prosperity to her people.

The mission to Punt had long-lasting effects. Earlier Egyptians had ventured there long before Hatshepsut's men did. But by her lifetime, it was a mysterious and unexplored land. The safe return of her ships proved she had established friendly trade and relations with the people of Punt. She was the first of the New Kingdom to do so, and it inspired later pharaohs—including Thutmose III—to follow her lead.

Inscriptions show that Hatshepsut waged war against Nubia, located south of Egypt, but some historians are skeptical. Some inscriptions refer to Hatshepsut engaging in battle herself: "I followed the good god, the King of Upper and Lower Egypt, Maatkare, may she live! I saw him [Hatshepsut] overthrowing the Nubian nomads, their chiefs being brought to him as prisoners. I saw him destroying the land of Nubia while I was in the following of His Majesty." Some historians think this story was borrowed from earlier Egyptian warriors.

9 CHAPTER

REMOVING HATSHEPSUT FROM HISTORY

 festoon

For the archaeologists who uncovered Djeser-Dje-seru during the last half of the 1800s, the site was an amazing find. But in the 1920s, an even more dramatic discovery was made at Deir el Bahri. In that decade, a team of Egyptologists from New York City's Metropolitan Museum of Art stumbled upon two huge quarries there.

The Egyptologists excavated about 200 statues carved in Hatshepsut's image. They also found several huge temple sphinxes whose faces also bore her image. But these massive sculptures were not discovered whole. Rather, they had been viciously attacked and thrown into the pits. Pieces ranged from shards of marble the size of a little finger to huge chunks of sandstone weighing a ton or more.

Thutmose III was one of the greatest military pharaohs of ancient Egypt.

The destruction was enormous. Heads had been hacked from the stone bodies. In most cases, the statues' eyes had been gouged out and some of the faces smashed. The royal uraeus had been smashed from the statues' foreheads. Later, archaeologists began to find further acts of destruction against Hatshepsut's images. On temple walls, monuments, and stelae of all kinds, her name and image had been scratched out, covered over, or otherwise defaced.

For those early 20th century Egyptologists, what had happened was obvious. Enraged at having been denied his rightful role as pharaoh by his "detested stepmother," they said, Thutmose III went on a rampage of revenge as soon as she died. He had

The image of Hatshepsut (middle) in the Karnak temple was scraped from the stone.

acted out his hatred against Hatshepsut throughout Egypt. These Egyptologists sided with Thutmose and viewed Hatshepsut and her actions in the worst possible light.

Referring to Hatshepsut's "theft" of the throne, Egyptologist William C. Hayes wrote in 1953, "It was not long ... before this vain, ambitious, and unscrupulous woman showed herself in her true colors." Even earlier, other well-established Egyptologists and historians expressed a similar perspective. One of these, James H. Breasted, wrote that during Hatshepsut's reign, "the conventions of the court were all warped and distorted to suit the rule of a woman."

Among modern Egyptologists, this view of the relationship between Hatshepsut and Thutmose III has lost its momentum. No evidence has been found of any feud, rebellion, or even unfriendly relations between the pharaoh and her stepson. Egyptologists do agree, though, that it was primarily Thutmose III who attempted to wipe out all record of Hatshepsut.

There was probably a good reason Hatshepsut did not simply hand the throne over to Thutmose III when he came of age. This possible reason is found in the ancient Egyptian belief system. During coronation, the divine royal ka entered into the pharaoh, making him no longer merely human. With this godlike element added, he could no more stop being king than he could stop being an Egyptian by birth.

Pharaohs ruled until death. So stepping down was probably not an option for Hatshepsut.

In regnal year 22, Thutmose III proclaimed himself sole ruler of Upper and Lower Egypt. This leads Egyptologists to believe that Hatshepsut must have died by that year. She was probably in her mid-50s —considered well into old age for that time period.

Contrary to earlier theories about him, Thutmose III was apparently content with being a co-regent. He was general of the army when he ruled with Hatshepsut and could have attempted to dethrone her at any time, but he did not. In more recent years, inscriptions have been found proving that he did not carry out his acts of destruction until about 20 years after Hatshepsut's death.

If the destruction of Hatshepsut's monuments was an act of fury, why did Thutmose wait so long? Few traces of rivalry—if any—can be found between the two rulers. Therefore, many modern Egyptologists believe that Thutmose III accepted his secondary position behind Hatshepsut and trained for military leadership that would benefit him when he became pharaoh.

One of the most important parts of his training was learning how to handle horses. The Egyptian military depended on horses for its superior battle power, and soldiers learned to be expert horsemen. Thutmose also had to be highly skilled at driving chariots and using weapons of all kinds.

The military training was useful when Thutmose III became pharaoh, and he became the greatest conqueror Egypt had ever seen. His military conquests surpassed those of his grandfather and great grandfather, resulting in a more powerful Egypt.

His son, Amenhotep II, would naturally expect to inherit the throne. But as the end of Thutmose's life grew nearer, the pharaoh may have been worried that his son would not become ruler. This is one reason Thutmose III may have tried to remove Hatshepsut from history. By removing his stepmother's name

Amenhotep II is thought to have ruled Egypt for about 27 years (c. 1427–1400 B.C.).

from the list of kings he compiled, he would appear in history as Thutmose II's only successor. This would strengthen his son Amenhotep II's case to become pharaoh if others tried to take over after Thutmose III's death. If viewed this way, all of this destruction was done to ensure his son's claim to the throne.

Historians suspect there is another reason for Thutmose's actions. Hatshepsut's 20-year reign was characterized by peace, prosperity, exploration of distant lands, and building projects that far outdid those of many male pharaohs. Each of her accomplishments boosted her reputation, which may have led Thutmose III to wipe her out of history.

Hatshepsut had proved that a woman could command a powerful country. Thutmose III may have wanted to ward off the possibility of female rulers in the future. By destroying evidence of a successful female ruler, the traditional male role of the pharaoh would be re-established. Without such a female role model, future generations of women would maintain their traditional places in society.

Indications that this may have been Thutmose's primary motivation are found in the selective way he attempted to rewrite history. He ordered the destruction of Hatshepsut's name and images only where they showed her to be king. Her portrayals as the God's Wife of Amen or as queen were left untouched.

Thutmose also may have tried to pull down the gigantic obelisks at Karnak. These monuments, however, would not fall. Writings on one portion of the monuments indicate Hatshepsut may have worried about what would occur after her death. "Now my heart turns this way and that," she wrote, "as I think what the people will say—those who shall see my monuments in years to come and who shall speak of what I have done."

Some Egyptologists believe that Thutmose III hid the obelisks by walling them up because he could not destroy them. One of the obelisks eventually crumbled on its own,

Ancient remains show that Thutmose III tried to take credit for many of Hatshepsut's works. He had a new quartzite sarcophagus carved for Thutmose I, replacing the one Hatshepsut had made. He also built a chapel to Hathor on top of the one Hatshepsut had built. He raised two giant obelisks—though not as big as hers—in front of the wall that was hiding hers. He claimed to have built two giant pylons that Hatshepsut had actually built. He erected statues of himself to replace similar ones depicting Hatshepsut. He also copied her by claiming the god Amen chose him to rule. He even added words to his monuments that closely copied those Hatshepsut had used in describing herself and her achievements.

but the other remained standing. In the 1800s, when the wall was pulled down, there stood a detailed testament to Hatshepsut's incredible reign. The name that had been lost for more than 3,000 years had come to light.

The reasons Thutmose III acted as he did will probably remain a mystery, and many other questions still surround Hatshepsut and the people who were close to her. For instance, what was her relationship with Senenmut? Was he simply a trusted adviser, or was their relationship also romantic, as some evidence suggests? Senenmut never married and had no children, which was unusual in ancient Egypt.

Senenmut's works and name are everywhere. After building himself a mortuary tomb earlier in his career, he later created a new, grander one. Located directly beneath Djeser-Djeseru, the tomb was more magnificent than that of even some pharaohs. Senenmut could not have completed such a major building project without Hatshepsut—and others—being aware of it. For a non-royal citizen to have such a lavish mortuary tomb, especially in such close proximity to that of a king, would have been unheard of. That Hatshepsut apparently gave her consent for this project indicates his significant importance to her.

Senenmut's name also appears with Hatshepsut's on some monuments. Most of these inscriptions are informal and do not display the kind of professional

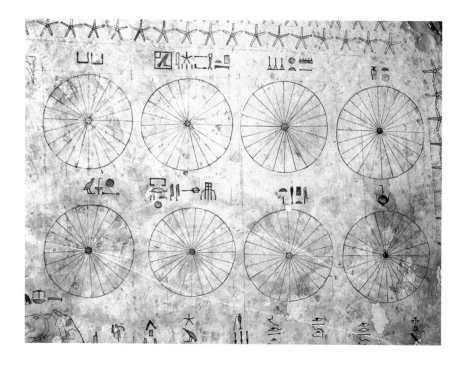

relationship that might be expected. Their names have also been found carved together on small devotional objects.

The last time Senenmut's name appears is dated from Hatshepsut's regnal year 16. No later inscriptions exist. After years of devotion and service to Hatshepsut, he suddenly disappears from all records.

Something strange must have happened. Senenmut was never buried in either of his tombs. His unfinished sarcophagus was found in the second tomb in the 1900s, but most of its other furnishings had been looted long before. The exquisite walls and ceiling had been defiled, and the entrance to the

Areas of the ceiling of Senenmut's tomb are beautifully painted with constellations, such as Orion, and the planets Venus, Mercury, Saturn, and Jupiter. The tomb's astronomical ceiling is the oldest "star map" ever found.

Senenmut's second tomb brings up mysterious questions about him even today. Was it a secret construction project? It seems almost impossible, but the tomb's entrance was hidden deep in a quarry that was providing stone for some of Hatshepsut's building projects. The fact that he built it so close to Hatshepsut's mortuary temple shows the kind of extraordinary relationship they must have had. The tomb itself is also quite extraordinary. Even though it was never completed, it is brilliantly designed, showing off Senenmut's dramatic vision and architectural genius.

chamber in which he would have been buried was found entirely sealed, with workmen's tools still inside. Senenmut's mummy has never been identified.

An attempt was also made to wipe out Senenmut's name and image in numerous places after his death. This occurred not only in his own tombs, but within the temple walls of Djeser-Djeseru as well. The damage was not consistent, though. Sometimes both his name and his image were hacked out. In other places, it was just one or the other. A few inscriptions and images of himself that Senenmut cleverly hid have survived intact, including at least one in full color hidden within Djeser-Djeseru.

Several of Hatshepsut's other officials suffered the same fate. The tomb walls of her high priest Hapuseneb, her treasurer Thuty, and at least three other loyal men of her court were similarly defaced. Their names—along with Hatshepsut's—were scraped away from inscriptions. Prayers and words of high praise for her were destroyed as well.

Whoever ordered these acts must have wanted Hatshepsut's trusted advisers forgotten, just as they hoped she would be. But not everyone in Hatshepsut's court mysteriously disappeared, and not all of their monuments were defiled. Some served Thutmose III for many years afterward.

As for Hatshepsut, what occurred between regnal year 17 and year 22 is unclear. No records remain, and the secrets lie buried. The questions are nearly endless and may never be answered. ॐ

10 DISCOVERING A LOST PHARAOH

❧

One of Hatshepsut's greatest mysteries kept Egyptologists searching for decades: the location of her mummy. She chose to build her burial tomb in Wadi Gabbanat el-Qurud, a desert region west of the Nile River. There, dry riverbeds called wadis cut into the cliffs. At the base of one of the cliffs, a wide crack in the stone provided a way into the mountainside.

It seemed a perfect place to hide a queen and her valuables after death. No other tombs existed nearby, so tomb robbers would not have been lured there. Even if thieves did venture into the wadis, finding the tomb's entrance would be difficult.

Although only a queen then, Hatshepsut was already doing things differently. It was uncommon for a pharaoh to select a burial spot away from those of other royals. But she was following her father, who had first selected a burial spot far from earlier pharaohs. Later pharaohs chose to be buried along with Thutmose I in what is known today as the Valley of the Kings. No other queens chose to be buried in the wadi that Hatshepsut had chosen.

Hatshepsut's first tomb was unlike any before it. A stairway at the entrance led down to a long corridor that ended in a single room. A second, shorter corridor led to the right, where a second room had been carved out of the rock. A unique feature of the second room was a passageway that led even deeper to yet another room.

In 1916, archaeologists found Hatshepsut's yellow quartzite queen's sarcophagus in this third room. The empty sarcophagus, engraved with her name and titles, was positioned to be hauled down to its final resting place. But the sarcophagus never got there. The tomb had been abandoned. A king needed a pharaoh's tomb that reflected a high status—the tomb of a mere queen would not do for Hatshepsut.

For her pharaoh's tomb site, Hatshepsut chose a spot closer to that of her father. She was entitled to be buried in the Valley of the Kings, and she selected a place on its east side. Her tomb is the longest and deepest in the entire valley: an underground tunnel 656 feet (200 m) long ending in three small chambers.

In 1799, an expedition sent by Napoléon to Egypt reported seeing the entrance to Hatshepsut's tomb. The leader of a French archaeological expedition recorded seeing the entrance in 1817. In 1903 and 1904, famed Egyptologist Howard Carter managed to clear the tomb's blocked passageways. He labeled it KV20.

The tomb had been ransacked long before. Some items remained, including two yellow quartzite

Howard Carter (seated) also discovered the tomb of the famous King Tutankhamen.

sarcophagi. One was inscribed with Hatshepsut's titles as king. The second had displayed her cartouches as well, but it had been altered to fit a larger body and reinscribed with the pharaonic names of Thutmose I. Carter also discovered canopic jars—containers that held a mummy's most important bodily organs.

Carter's opinion was that Thutmose I built the tomb, but Hatshepsut decided to use it as a joint burial place for the two of them. Other scholars believe it had always been Hatshepsut's tomb and she had her father's sarcophagus moved to be with her own. Modern Egyptologists think that KV20 began as Thutmose II's tomb but was taken over by Hatshepsut upon his death. The three chambers may have been burial chambers for Hatshepsut, her father, and her brother/husband.

Hatshepsut's sarcophagus, which was recut for her father, can be seen at the Museum of Fine Arts in Boston.

Whomever tomb KV20 was originally intended for, it was empty of bodies when Carter investigated it. Hatshepsut's sarcophagus was empty and had never been used. Hatshepsut's mummy was still missing.

But in 1903, Carter discovered another tomb near KV20 labeled KV60. It turned out to belong to Hatshepsut's childhood nurse, Sitre, or Inet. Two female mummies were found inside. At the time, most Egyptologists assumed one of them was Sitre because it was found in a sarcophagus inscribed with her name. But because of its small, delicate bone structure and "royal looking face," other Egyptologists thought it might be Hatshepsut.

The other mummy was lying on its back on the floor. The body was of an overweight woman about 5 feet (150 centimeters) tall. The mummy's teeth were badly worn, and only a few long strands of her reddish-gold hair remained. The body was partially unwrapped, but her left arm was lying diagonally across her chest with the hand in a fist, a typical pose for royal mummies.

Carter left the two mummies where they were and sealed the tomb. In 1908, another Egyptologist removed Sitre and her sarcophagus to the Cairo museum. No one paid much attention to the remaining mummy because the tomb was not a royal one, and there was no way to identify the remaining body.

Decades passed as Egyptologists continued to

speculate on the identity of the mummy in KV60. In the 2000s, Zahi Hawass, secretary general of the Supreme Council of Antiquities in Cairo, took the mummy out of the tomb to see what he could determine about it. His discovery rocked the world of Egyptology.

In June 2007, Hawass announced that Hatshepsut had been positively identified using the latest scientific technology. The mummy found more than 100 years earlier on the floor of an obscure tomb was Hatshepsut. It was the most important find since the discovery of King Tutankhamen's tomb in the 1920s.

Scientists had little doubt when it came to identifying Hatshepsut's mummified remains. The biggest clue was found in a canopic jar bearing her cartouche. A CT scan revealed that inside the sealed jar was the pharaoh's liver and one of her molars. Further CT scans showed that the unidentified mummy was missing a molar. When a dentist measured the tooth and the empty spot in the mummy's jaw, he found a perfect fit. Because the size, shape, and placement of everyone's teeth are unique, this was convincing evidence that the body was Hatshepsut. Examination of the mummy also revealed that Hatshepsut was suffering from cancer, which may have been the cause of her death.

To be left alone on the floor of a humble tomb seems an undignified end for a female ruler. But Hatshepsut's efforts as pharaoh were not in vain. Although most traces of her life, her name, and her

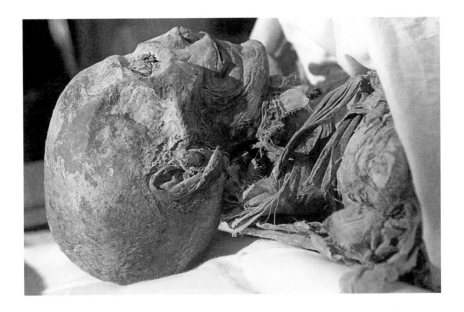

After being
positively
identified,
Hatshepsut's
mummy was
put on display
at the Cairo
Museum in
Egypt.

triumphs were nearly erased from history, modern scientists have rescued her from that fate. Scientists feel certain that Hatshepsut has now been positively identified, but they are still curious about her heritage. They plan to compare samples of Hatshepsut's DNA with samples from the mummies of her father, Thutmose I, her grandmother Ahmose-Nefertari, and her childhood nanny, Sitre.

Hatshepsut clearly worried how—and if—she would be remembered. On the obelisk still standing at Karnak, she left a prayer that was never destroyed. That prayer was "that her name might remain enduring in this temple forever and ever." Although nearly forgotten, the name Maatkare Hatshepsut, King of Upper and Lower Egypt, does indeed still live. ✏

HATSHEPSUT'S LIFE

C. 1550 B.C.

Start of New
Kingdom and
18th dynasty

1550 B.C.

1557 B.C.

Memphis, capital
of Lower Egypt,
becomes the largest
city in the world

1523 B.C.

Shang dynasty begins
in ancient China

WORLD EVENTS

EARLY 1500S B.C.

Birth of Hatshepsut, probably before Thutmose I became pharaoh

1504 B.C.

Hatshepsut's father, Thutmose I, becomes pharaoh; Thutmose II is born around this time

1505 B.C.

1506 B.C.

Cecrops, legendary king of Athens, dies after a 50-year reign

C. 1504 B.C.

Polynesians settle in Fiji

HATSHEPSUT'S LIFE

C. 1492 B.C.

Death of Thutmose I;
Thutmose II
becomes pharaoh

1500 B.C.

C. 1500 B.C.

Corn farmers settle near
the Rio Grande in what
is now the southwest
United States

1480 B.C.

Hurrians from the Zagros
Mountains overrun and
dominate the Assyrians

WORLD EVENTS

1479 B.C.

Death of Thutmose II;
Thutmose III becomes
pharaoh; Hatshepsut
begins ruling Egypt as
his regent

1475 B.C.

Hatshepsut sends
trading expedition
to Punt

1475 B.C.

C. **1475** B.C.

According to the
Bible, Moses leads
exodus of Jews from
slavery in Egypt

HATSHEPSUT'S LIFE

C. 1473 B.C.

Hatshepsut claims
pharaoh status and
jointly rules with
Thutmose III

1459 B.C.

Last dated
reference to
Hatshepsut as
pharaoh

1460 B.C.

1472 B.C.

Danaus becomes
king of Argos in
what is now Greece

1460 B.C.

Hittite Empire
controls what
is now Turkey

WORLD EVENTS

C. 1457 B.C.

Last possible year of
Hatshepsut's and Thutmose
III's joint rule, meaning
Hatshepsut has died

1450 B.C.

1446 B.C.

The Pentateuch—the
first five books of the
Bible—are written

1450 B.C.

Mycenaean Greeks
conquer Minoan
civilization on Crete

PRENOMEN:	Maatkare
NOMEN:	Hatshepsut
DATE OF BIRTH:	c. early 1500s B.C.
BIRTHPLACE:	Probably royal city of Thebes, Egypt
FATHER:	Thutmose I
MOTHER:	Ahmose
SPOUSE:	Thutmose II
DATE OF MARRIAGE:	c. 1492 B.C.
CHILD:	Neferure
DATE OF DEATH:	c. 1457
MUMMY IDENTIFIED:	June 2007

Further Reading

Galford, Ellen. *Hatshepsut: The Princess Who Became King*. Washington, D.C.: National Geographic Children's Books, 2007.

Hawass, Zahi. *Curse of the Pharaohs: My Adventures With Mummies*. Washington, D.C.: National Geographic Society, 2004.

Adams, Simon, and Kent Weeks. *Ancient Egypt*. New York: Kingfisher, 2006.

Thomas, Susanna. *Hatshepsut: The First Woman Pharaoh*. New York: The Rosen Publishing Group, 2003.

Look for more Signature Lives books about this era:

Alexander the Great: *World Conqueror*

Aristotle: *Philosopher, Teacher, and Scientist*

Confucius: *Chinese Philosopher and Teacher*

Hypatia: *Mathematician, Inventor, and Philosopher*

Julius Caesar: *Roman General and Statesman*

Ramses II: *Egyptian Pharaoh, Warrior, and Builder*

Socrates: *Ancient Greek in Search of Truth*

Thucydides: *Ancient Greek Historian*

On the Web

For more information on this topic, use FactHound.

1. Go to *www.facthound.com*
2. Type in this book ID: 0756538351
3. Click on the *Fetch It* button.

FactHound will find the best Web sites for you.

Historic Sites

Cairo Egyptian Museum
Midan El Tahrir
Cairo, Egypt 11557
20-2-578-2448
Jewelry, sculpture, and other artifacts; also statuary and an entire room of mummies, including those of 18th dynasty pharaohs and many other figures from ancient Egypt

Metropolitan Museum of Art
1000 Fifth Ave.
New York, NY 10028
212/535-7710
Statues of Hatshepsut and many other artifacts from ancient Egyptian life

cartouche

in Egyptian hieroglyphs, an oval shape that represents a loop of rope tied at the ends; contains a pharaoh's royal name

colonnade

hallway-shaped structure supported by columns, creating an open walkway

coronation

ceremony of crowning a king or queen

crook

long stick, or staff, with a curved end that was used by shepherds; along with the flail, the crook was a symbol of the pharaoh's power

excavated

dug up or removed from the ground

flail

short, wood-handled tool used in ancient Egypt to separate seeds from harvested grains, and carried by the pharaoh as a symbol of power

hieroglyphics

having to do with hieroglyphs

hieroglyphs

symbols used to write the ancient Egyptian language

ka

ancient Egyptian name for the soul—the formless aspect of a person that survived death to live in the afterlife

maat

in ancient Egypt, the natural, cosmic, and divine order of the universe

mortuary temple

in ancient Egypt, a temple built to worship a pharaoh's chosen deities and to commemorate the pharaoh's reign before and after his death

nemes
striped royal headdress worn by a pharaoh

obelisks
tall, square-based columns that taper to a point at the top

pharaonic
having to do with the pharaohs

portico
covered porchlike area surrounded by columns that support the roof

regalia
in ancient Egypt, a group of objects—such as a crook, flail, double crown, and false beard—that symbolized the pharaoh's position and power

regnal
relating to a king's ascension to the throne

reliefs
sculptures carved on a wall or other surface using techniques that create raised images against a flat background

sarcophagus
stone coffin inscribed with carved words and images

sphinxes
stone statues having a human head atop the body of a resting lion

stelae
carved or inscribed stone pillars or slabs, usually created in ancient times to make important events known

uraeus
carved snake's head displayed on the royal headdress of a pharaoh as a symbol of absolute power

Chapter 2

Page 25, line 1: Joyce Tyldesley. *Hatchepsut: The Female Pharaoh.* London: Penguin Group, 1996, p. 103.

Page 25, line 6: Michael Hayes. *The Egyptians.* New York: Rizzoli, 1998, p. 97.

Page 26, line 9: *Hatchepsut: The Female Pharaoh,* p. 104.

Chapter 4

Page 39, line 1: Ibid., p. 70.

Page 40, line 23: Evelyn Wells. *Hatshepsut.* Garden City, N.Y.: Doubleday & Company, Inc., 1969, p. 154.

Page 43, line 15: *Hatchepsut: The Female Pharaoh,* p. 88

Chapter 5

Page 49, line 1: Catharine H. Roehrig. *Hatshepsut: From Queen to Pharaoh.* New York: The Metropolitan Museum of Art, 2005, p. 297.

Page 50, line 11: *Hatchepsut: The Female Pharaoh,* pp. 97–98.

Chapter 6

Page 58, line 5: James Henry Breasted, ed. *Ancient Records of Egypt,* vol 2. Urbana: University of Illinois Press, 2001, p. 231.

Chapter 7

Page 63, line 2: *Hatshepsut,* p. 193.

Page 63, line 6: Ibid., pp. 193–94.

Page 64, sidebar: Alexandre Moret. *Kings and Gods of Egypt.* New York: G.P. Putnam's Sons, 1912, p. 37.

Page 69, sidebar: *Hatshepsut: From Queen to Pharaoh,* p. 84.

Page 69, line 17: James B. Pritchard, ed. *The Ancient Near East.* Princeton, N.J.: Princeton University Press, 1969, p. 231.

Chapter 8

Page 73, line 5: *Hatshepsut,* p. 243.

Page 75, sidebar: *Hatchepsut: The Female Pharaoh,* p. 143.

Chapter 9

Page 79, line 6: *Hatshepsut: From Queen to Pharaoh,* p. 297.

Page 79, line 12: Ibid.

Page 83, line 20: Elizabeth B. Wilson. "The Queen Who Would Be King." *Smithsonian.* Sept. 2006. 15 Aug. 2007. www.smithsonianmag.com/history-archaeology/hatshepsut.html?c=y&page=5

Chapter 10

Page 95, line 12: *Hatshepsut,* p. 259.

Breasted, James Henry, ed. *Ancient Records of Egypt*, vol 2. Urbana: University of Illinois Press, 2001.

Dersin, Denise, ed. *What Life Was Like on the Banks of the Nile: Egypt 3050 BC–30 BC.* Alexandria, Va.: Time-Life Books, 1997.

El Mahdy, Christine. *Tutankhamen: The Life and Death of the Boy King.* New York: St. Martin's Press, 1999.

Johnson, Paul. *The Civilization of Ancient Egypt.* New York: Harper Collins, 1998.

Hayes, Michael. *The Egyptians.* New York: Rizzoli, 1998.

Hobson, Christine. *The World of the Pharaohs: A Complete Guide to Ancient Egypt.* New York: Thames & Hudson, Inc., 1997.

Karlson, Jane. "Hatshepsut, Queen of Egypt, 1504–1482 BC." *The Web Chronology Project.* 8 May 1998. 22 Sept. 2006. www.thenagain.info/WebChron/Africa/Hatshepsut.html

Montet, Pierre. *Lives of the Pharaohs.* New York: The World Publishing Company, 1968.

Moret, Alexandre. *Kings and Gods of Egypt.* New York: G.P. Putnam's Sons, 1912.

Pritchard, James B., ed. *The Ancient Near East.* Princeton, N.J.: Princeton University Press, 1969.

Roehrig, Catharine H. *Hatshepsut: From Queen to Pharaoh.* New York: The Metropolitan Museum of Art, 2005.

Shaw, Ian. *Exploring Ancient Egypt.* Oxford, England: Oxford University Press, 2003.

Tyldesley, Joyce. *Hatchepsut: The Female Pharaoh.* London: Penguin Group, 1996.

Wells, Evelyn. *Hatshepsut.* Garden City, N.Y.: Doubleday & Company, Inc., 1969.

Wilson, Elizabeth B. "The Queen Who Would Be King." *Smithsonian.* Sept. 2006. 15 Aug. 2007. www.smithsonianmag.com/history-archaeology/hatshepsut.html?c=y&page=5

Pamela Dell began her professional career writing for adults and started writing for children about 12 years ago. Since then she has published fiction and nonfiction books, written numerous magazine articles, and created award-winning interactive multimedia.

Image Credits